Praise for Uncomfortable Minds

"Larry Sorkin's new book of poems *Uncomfortable Minds* brings to us many forms of solace and questioning—reflections both bitter and tangy, sweet and unbearable. The term 'uncomfortable minds' is Larry's riff on an e.e. cummings quote about 'Cambridge ladies who… are unbeautiful and have comfortable minds.' Larry's poems shoulder us into various forms of discomfort or surprise. One poem begins with confronting a raccoon and leads into a literally touching father-son connection. He wryly confronts the Founding Fathers' promise of 'happiness' and finds he's been waiting for a refund. And what about poetry itself? Larry is a wonderful discoverer of poetry. He has read widely and often communicates what he has discovered, spreading the word of its wonder in many arenas. He says of poetry 'Doesn't it only/transform when/ it strikes the just /so chord along the sound / board (and here comes the surprise) of my crooked spine.' Notice the inventiveness of those line breaks! It seems he wants the reader to consider waking from illusion, but also from disillusion. He is deeply fond of attachments. Talking about being deeply connected to a place, he says 'Fuck/ holy detachment.' There are many memorable images. And finally, he welcomes the comforts of memory which shines in its bright and fragmented way through so much of his work."

> —**Lou Lipsitz**, *Seeking the Hook, if this world falls apart*

"Out of a richly lived and deeply spiritual life, Sorkin's restless mind plays up and down each linguistically artful occasionally profane page. Populated with fauna and familiars, both living and dead, these sometimes-joyful elegies—spoken with fearlessness and a touch of cynicism—take me by surprise, no matter how many times I reread them. Reader, these Uncomfortable Minds will move, disturb, and delight. Dig in."

> —**Roger Weingarten**, *The Four Gentlemen and their Footman, Premature Elegy by Firelight*

UNCOMFORTABLE
MINDS

UNCOMFORTABLE
MINDS

POEMS
LARRY SORKIN

bonhomie 🍐 press

CORAL GABLES

Cover & Layout Design: Carmen Fortunato
Cover Photo: Mari Feni, Milan
Author's Photo: Deborah Mulcahy

For permission requests, please contact the publisher at:
Mango Publishing Group
2850 S Douglas Road, 2nd Floor
Coral Gables, FL 33134 USA
info@mango.bz

For special orders, quantity sales, course adoptions and corporate sales, please email
the publisher at sales@mango.bz. For trade and wholesale sales, please contact Ingram
Publisher Services at customer.service@ingramcontent.com or +1.800.509.4887.

Uncomfortable Minds: Poems

Library of Congress Cataloging-in-Publication number: 2020951186
ISBN: (print) 978-1-64250-525-2, (ebook) 978-1-64250-526-9
BISAC category code POE000000   POETRY / General

Printed in the United States of America

In memory of my mother, Selma

TABLE OF CONTENTS

ACKNOWLEDGMENTS

I wish to thank the editors and authors of the following books, anthologies, journals and organizations that have published or recognized my poems in various versions in the following:

The Undertaker's Daughter, Gallery Books: "Two Weeks in the Ground."

…and love…, Jacar Press: "Think."

Men of Their Word, Triangle Men's Center: "My Father Was the Sea."

What Matters, Jacar Press: "She Started with the Question."

Poetry's Lighthouse, CreateSpace Independent Publishing Platform: "Forgettable Chat," "Loosely Tied," "All Night the Wind."

Interpoezia: "Pursuit," "Call Me Adam," "Simple Prayer," "She Calls Me When I Am Out."

Kakalak 2014: "Your Private Ocean," 2015: "Doubletake," 2016: "Buzzard Luck" (Honorable Mention), "Reading Obits."

Main Street Rag: "Two Sassy Women."

North Carolina Poetry Society, Poet Laureate Award Finalists: "Fish That Fly," *"Methinks my own soul must be a bright invisible green*—Thoreau."

While it's true that writing is a solitary and introspective art, it can have a strong social aspect as well through mentoring relationships, workshops, critique groups, and finding community in an audience. My own writing takes place in concert with others and to that end, I want to thank all those who have had a hand in these words.

Foremost, Roger Weingarten who has been teacher, mentor, friend, co-creator, editor and producer to these poems. He has been an exceptional help in allowing this manuscript to find its voice. With some of these poems, his critique has been limited to a line break or a word suggestion. More often, his radical revisioning has brought the pieces effectively to light. With every edit, I ask the poem what it wants and almost universally, it welcomes his suggestions that have an uncanny way of revealing direction and insight. I am grateful and fortunate to have had his help.

For almost twenty years, I have had the benefit of sharing my work in what Henry Berne called his Poetry and Healing Group. I am grateful to all who have come and gone from these sessions. The Third Tuesday Davidson critique group has gone on almost as long with thanks to Don Carroll, Gilda Morina Syverson, Suzanne Leitner, Ann Campenella, Bob Cumming, Lou Green, Brenda Graham and Tootsie O'Hare. Thanks to Lou Lipsitz, Sarah Dimont Sorkin, Gail Peck and Diana Pinckney for helping edit and review the manuscript and to Nora Ligorano for help with graphic design. Thanks too to Leslie Ullman, David Wojahn and groups at Vermont College of Fine Arts for advice and critique. Thanks to Barbara Buckman Strasko for suggesting the title, though it's not surprising that I've never become "comfortable" with it. I'm indebted to Mitchell Kaplan and Books & Books for all their faith and patience. Thanks to Yaddyra Peralta and the folks at Mango Publishing and Bonhomie Press for getting the book to the finishing line in its publishing journey. To my brother Steve, sister Judy and son Mica for loving support and encouragement. Always I'm grateful and uncannily lucky to have Brenda, my wife and muse, beside me.

ONE

MASQUERADE

To pretend is to know oneself
—Pessoa

He poses wilted
roses in hand to be Husband
to his wife, been trying on that
persona for years though rarely
fools himself let alone
the lovely woman who humors his
attempts. He puts on the requisite

uniform of Businessman and steps
into an office where staff pretend
they know him as he struts, issues orders, puts
on a serious face before declaring
an important meeting and goes
home for a nap. Surely,
in the privacy of his room, he
can convince himself it's not
an act, then dreams of becoming a Red

Tailed Hawk's drift and call
over undulating hills. He's January
Rain, plunging through freezing
air, then ice that
shatters, melts and seeps
into dirt. Awake, buoyed, he

can be Anything, Anyone. In his garage,
he decides to impersonate Small
Engine Mechanic—isn't every man
born skilled in such? Chainsaw seeing
through his ruse refuses
to start.

Larry Sorkin

Skeptic

The psychic—who must have watched my eyes
roll through the phone—makes

it clear I'm invited to her brunch
provided I embrace

the theme of the ever-so-
popular and amazing faith-

healer-mystic-channeling-South
American-ambassador of—you

guessed it—Señor God. Skeptical
me could probably fake it if the attendees weren't,

to a woman, all intuitives who'd
know of the ruse and why would I want

to be there, except perhaps there's
something I need to learn in that bagels

and cream cheese milieu of love
and light. So I check my gut which gurgles

ambivalence and then consult
the I-Ch'ing which says in no

certain terms to stay clear of the who-
do-voodoo and keep

both my size fifteen sandals firmly
planted in the quick

sand of my own skeptical sex-
agenarian superstitions.

METHINKS MY OWN SOUL MUST BE A BRIGHT INVISIBLE GREEN—THOREAU

Visit with me at my
terraced garden faced
with rock, a few steps
from the kitchen door
beside a house dug
deep into a remote
forested hill and you
might guess at my emerald
soul. If so, you'd be
mistaken. Thoreau may
lay claim to such a verdant
interior but it's a stark
reflection I catch
in the mirror, a soul
grown up under TV
brilliance, nurtured
by plastic containers foraged
from supermarket aisles, days spent
zigzagging narrow
highway lanes over a tamed
landscape. Even these
few words input to hard
drive are no romantic
scribbles to a well-worn
journal. If you find me this
spring rooting in the soil, it's not
because I have the nature
of nature in my soul, but
because of its absence that
I reach for a handhold in this
dirt.

Larry Sorkin

FISH THAT FLY

birds that swim. In this
unlikely club, consider

the Anhinga. Slogging
through the Glades waist deep

she's perched above on a cypress, her serpent
neck, her reckless

plunge, a seeming
contradiction for one

shy even of land, choosing
to go to depths albeit in search

of a meal. There must
have been a first

time, a dive to a place of no
air, no sky: the long

held breath; webbing growing
between her toes. What

am I? What would I do
one morning, shoeless and hungry

at the edge of something
I couldn't explain?

Continuum

Connects two u's in such cozy
proximity, as though that was the most
normal thing. On the silhouette

of Boston's skyline from my plate
glass perch, two rusty cranes appear
to be dancing, their stretched steel

necks crossed in this long
distance illusion made possible by point
of view and wishful thinking—without

which it would just be urban
ugly. Everything finds its
place somewhere on that rosy

shifting line between say
loving concern and sociopathy. I maintain
the illusion I am colored that shade

of normal where I pass
a buck on to the bag lady on one
corner and evict a tenant from my bit above sub-

standard housing on the next. I place myself midpoint
at the dinner table: eschew four leggeds and those
with wings while devouring a bowl

of mussels in a divine
broth followed by flaky pan
seared cod. Without that solid bell

curve, I suspect I'd drown
in sensitivity and madness. Yet this
morning there's a disquiet. Something happened

in the night, the cranes have swung
apart on their base, busy lifting heavy
cement while I tread

water, my head just a hair
above the surface
far from land and life line.

THE KNOCK

Daybreak's flashy cardinal throwing
himself against my window tries

to rouse me. Minutes
pass while I ignore his call and dig

my head into the pillow before a sharp
thud drags me out of sleep to a goldfinch

on the deck, neck broken—a lemon
pixie flexing his tail, taking a last

breath. Dusk now,I wonder was I worth
the sacrifice? Did it

succeed in waking me? Did I
hear the knock?

Larry Sorkin

BOTHERED

by the dirt bike
brethren boy who'd
often take an afternoon

earsplitting buzz across the ridge
road forest track to terrify
whitetail that loved to plague

my vegetable garden. Even
letting treefall clog
the wagon road wouldn't

stop his teeny-
bopper lust to scar
the foliage and burst

into my clearing to drop
in with his bright-eyed easy
chatter. Thirty years later and the deer

herd's decimated—though
these days I'm too busy to bother
with even field mint—and the next

generation neighbor kids are lost
to their screens, and that
boy never made it

past eighteen. I have a rare
quiet moment on the porch. Shouldn't
I be content?

Ritual of the grand

jury in my rural county, heaven
and hell to a gossip, the worst/best

juice in gory detail that can't
be spoken outside this

sanctified room despite
the foregone

conclusion that we'll send each
matter over to

trial—forced to hear
of our sister

the thief, our brother who cooks
meth, neighbor who struck

his wife. We sit
in secret, everyman

chosen in random
lottery to hear

victim and offender spoken
in our chamber, sit

with the sacred
law, charges

written and sworn before
the deity by the uniformed

officers who describe
the act. We vote to have

our relations, we're all,
the Lakota say, related—go

to judgment, then hold these
secrets forever so the act,

the named and the state can carry
on with their commerce in the open

while we keep the messy
beauty in the locked

chest of our shamed
and saddened hearts.

LOONS, SHEARWATERS, TERNS

and cormorants: a feeding
floating congregation

bobs and dives into the glassy
calm with a bottlenose

dolphin that indulges
and sates on schooled, mirrored

muscle and flash. A brown
pelican gains altitude to glide

forever before its wing
tip nearly grazes a blossoming

wave: is it
true, despite my

suspicions, that delight underlies
everything?

Cambridge ladies and magic soap

*…Cambridge ladies who live in furnished souls are unbeautiful and
have comfortable minds*

—e. e. cummings

*…friend and enemy, the whole human race, the six billion strong, for
we're All-One or none…*

—Dr. Bronner Magic Soap label

thanks to too much time in the tub with dr. bronner I take
exception to e.e.'s exaggeration/characterization that any
creature however low could have a comfortable mind can't
you see the link between the u&me/the universal
each&every elephant to protozoa, wobbly
walkers/frog jumpers/school swimmers each
painted by the same restless
brush in that flawed image not
the whether but the how
of our missing/broken
parts our allthesame diversity in
the light from each&every
eye we see the unfinished
imperfect brokenness
of our uncomfortable
sister/brotherhood.

PEOPLE ARE ASSHOLES

for Jack

he declares as we dig into stone
crab bits poached in butter with
citrus and micro-greens—compliments

of his chef pal. A revelation...*just
don't like them—no reason not
to speak the truth.* He has

my attention. All
of them? *Almost half voted
for that GOP jerk off didn't*

*they—and a lot of those fuckers didn't
bother or were undecided, you can't
be undecided with a schmuck*

like that unless... the waiter
brings out an oyster
empanada: warm cakey crust with a shallot

and mushroom sauce—not
on the menu. *My dad's one, the meanest
old fart and an asshole. Why*

should I pretend otherwise? followed by conch
fritters fried in strips, tenderized, in a light
aioli.

WHAT MEN CARRY

Toes curled over the edge, eyes
inched tight at first light, lips
pursed, dream

dissolving in daybreak. If
I had the guts, I'd take
on a deeper question. Petty

cares all I can handle. What
deadline missed, what slip
of the tongue slight, what tide

of worry digests
the day and jiggers
my mind steeled to love

its task and nothing
else? Brenda in freshened
light. How can this

woman wake
smiling? What is it
I carry, burdened, close

to broken: weight
and gravity? Toes curled
over the maddened void where

2

I'm afraid to look. More likely: the man
is and isn't
a statistic. The setting: Formica

table, vacant
stare surrounded by November
fog that rows the night

conjuring: wife
who bailed with kid; his
dad already a suicide

at his age. Deadened, a month
behind on rent, she
most likely believes

he's a loser. Nam tunneling
behind his cornea drove
nightmares, the gun

under his pillow. At
the table, this
man crushes a can

of Schlitz. Because he's not
a woman, research says,
he's less likely

to complai
of depression; isn't he
lucky that way?

Larry Sorkin

SIMPLE PRAYER

Sizzling dress leans
over the café table and asks

Lothario if
there's anything you're

afraid of. He swirls his
pinot. Nothing—well

maybe heights. He doesn't
say he's afraid she won't

sleep with him and doesn't
have a clue he's afraid

she will. He'd always
had one room hidden behind

the other in his house. Usually his
parachute

trove of tricks worked: survival
iffy from day one, a baby

crying for milk until
blue. But he'd come this

far hadn't he: made
his wish, paid the bar

tab and, staring hard
into the Bermuda

Triangle between her eyes, held
his breath?

POETRY'S PROBLEM

So it's not
music. So it wants

to sing and can't. So it's
not a Klimt that

takes your breath before
you blink. Don't you have to get

it before you get it? How,
at the starting gate,

can you tell if it's a long
suffering memoir, flash

fiction fantasy, leftist political
diatribe, or the minimalist deep

image moment when moonlight hits
dew on the rail just

before daybreak? Doesn't it only
transform when

it strikes the just
so chord along the sound

board of my crooked spine. It
has to remind me her eyes

flashed with a green that was worth
the heartbreak of loving her, no matter

it ended badly outside a garage
studio in an electric storm.

Wet Dream of the Founding Fathers

Happiness
guaranteed or your
money back bellowed
from the amusement
park booth loud

speaker. Even if they'd
meant to say
satisfaction, the absurdity on
its face caught
without a thought to

careening rafts packed with
kids and grown up
kids barreling over
rapids, sprayed and tossed
in the roiling, faces

contorted in extremis
of glee
that sent my sad
sack dystopic
negativity into dare

I say *joy* as I
realize my whole three
ring life I've
been waiting for
a refund.

No God but God

I've heard it from minarets—lā
ilāha ill ā-llāh, there is no

God but God and I've stood
for it in the temple—*Adonoi*

Eloheinu Adonoi Echod, the Lord
our God, the Lord is One, but I'd

never heard it like this summer
night in my bedroom listening

to a chorus of cicadas
and katydids, a pulsing clamor

joined with all the other background
songs. How constant

the praise and complaint, cry
and laugh; swimming

in the hot
soup of sound, so

full, so
empty.

Larry Sorkin

NEITHER THIS, NOR THAT—UPANISHADS

Today I'm nagged by knowing
I don't. I've lost those few

words that
would unlock

the puzzle, set
right this finely

wrought chaos—aren't you
looking for this too, the lost

quote gone from
book or memory of

our conversations. Friend,
I know we won't

find it plowing
and pressing seeds

into dirt, not in scarlet
tomatoes that come

later, not even in
the fine meal

we'll make of them. Does it
matter? Join me

in the garden.

Buzzard Luck

Can't kill nothin' and nothin' will die.
for Nick H

Uncle Nick's story defines it, shut
up and stranded in a tank on a hill
in Korea, tracks shot off, allies
in retreat, unable to lock
the hatch, the enemy pulling
from above to drop
in a grenade, he and his mates below struggling
to hold it closed, reaching in the toolbox for an enormous
screwdriver, the perfect lever to hold
the hatch shut and then the recognition
that the tool in hand was built
in his father's, my grandfather's,
factory. What kind

of luck puts him in hell then bestows
such blessing? What

kind of fowl
grin graces the beak
of the Gods as they
break us, save us and cackle as we
give thanks for our luck? Last

night, a towering carrion bird
bursts in through a vision, gray
wings extended, gorging on
another's entrails. Who
will I be in this
play: buzzard, carcass, or just
a fool with mouth agape watching?

Armistice Day

Why don't we read
signs anymore? In early
times, even the loose

ragged guts of chickens
divined our fate. Eleven
a.m., November eleventh,

a rural road, rusted trees backdrop
open pasture. Radio
Voice tells me last night a killer

storm swept the country, dozens
died while I snored, ears
covered to howling

and shaking awnings. My car crests
the hill where—pairs
of legs pierce

the air—a bloated
cow rolled
on her back, stark

white against spent
charred clouds. I can't
forget this

omen delivered by lightning
in the dark. I tremble for
our fate.

Exhortations from on High

I dreamt myself seated
in synagogue with my brother who's
about to stand and levitate
toward the pulpit to present his
bar mitzvah spiel but we're both too
grown up. *It's time,*
he whispers, *I can't*
say what they want me to; it's
time to shake
it up, like JC knockin' over temple
tables. Dream
shift to Tracy

Ullman as the black
robed rabbi who grabs
the mike and starts
pacing around and calling like
Professor Harold
Hill the Music Man telling
us all to loosen up, drop
this solemnity bit and enjoy
what we got 'cause that's
what we got. She gets us
crying in the passion which
builds to a frenzy when she
turns and flips
up the back of her robe, strutting her
radiant bare tush before
all the tribes lost and otherwise

Larry Sorkin

booted and dragged into life. *This
is God*, she swears, *this
is religion*. I don't
know about my dream
brother, but she made
me a believer.

`

For Henry at 81

Just when it seems I live in blind
alleys walking bare
pavement buoyed only by the color

of newspaper fliers from big
box stores and rare
cemeteries visits to place

pebbles on the headstones
of my ancestors, my white
haired friend says *Look again*, and I

wake in a dream to find
a lion outside my window roaming
content in the tawny

veldt. New rooms
pop up in my house where old
loves walk through walls to cry

with me, no words
left but water
flows across the old

man's tile bath and down
the grates. We follow
the stream out

to a beach where breakers
roll in, roar
onto sand and there, behind us

on white salt flats, a flock
of black tailed gulls a thousand
strong land on my eyelids.

TWO

BIRTHDAY EVE

I would not be
had there not been: the flu
epidemic of 1918; the American
Indian genocide; Hitler. Nor
would I be: without
Grandma's icebox
cake; Mom's hazel
eyes; Dad's light
step on a certain
chill October evening.

YOUR PRIVATE OCEAN

brags the label of this Upper
East Side hotel's spa
treatment body lotion. Is there
something to it beyond a squeeze
bottle and puffery? Having
slathered my dry
February skin, dreary as this
sleepless city, hyper
aware how alone: private
as in privation, next to the room
service menu, a gloss
glamour mag's buffed
blond clinks blued
martinis with her musk
doused boy. Are they
kidding? Escape
along the street finds
a briny collection of snow
capped garbage, buoys in the sea
of turned heads like yours
truly: roughened, un
beautiful, cocooned
and drifting. If there's a child
in me still, then mine
remembers being born to an accidental
family of random disconnect. Who were those
strangers? A contrast—my own
visage in every face. Can there
ever be a stranger? I've cleaned
toilets like the Rico
Tica angel who folded
down my bed, I've shimmied

　　　　　Larry Sorkin

through a too tight crawl
space like the coveralled
plumber in line with me for a sesame
bagel. I've devoted decades to filling
ledgers like the Second Avenue Brooks
Brothers dandy sprinting
past me for a cab. Mine
are their worn and sallow
eyes—alive long enough to fathom these
roots to my sister blocks away, rushing
to her as if I'm the one
trussed to the operating theater
stage where a mechanical snake worms between
our ribs to devour shards
of cancered lung. As kids we had
rivalry, distances and our odd
cloistered intimacy—is it easier
to love her as a stranger, so
isolated, close,
tethered and adrift, splayed
open, floating
on anesthesia?

...BURDEN AND TENDERNESS...
—MANDELSTAM

Siblings morph, kid's
jealousies become adult
resentment. Even if we get

along, reasons will
surface: luck,
money, fill

in the blank. Not with us. Dig
this unexpected contrary
destiny: together

in a tony
tropical café, the three
of us share a slice

of lemon ricotta
something like
Grandma's from a million

years ago. I want more—not
the pastry—but these
moments we can't

stop from dissolving, time
we won't
have again as

brother, sister, only
beginning to relish this
tenderness. Who

were we when days spread
forever past
the horizon?

Larry Sorkin

Family Restaurant on New Year's Day

When the dead come back it's
easy to forget they
were even there but
not last night's dream when we
sit down with long
dead grandparents in one
of those egg salad-on-toast-and-coffee
corner restaurants where
we jabber through the meal like
it's something we do every night until it's
over and the living
leave through the front while the dead
file out through swinging
kitchen doors. I follow
to a bench where Grandma sits somber
and quiet, as if waiting
for a bus. I kneel,
touch her forehead with
mine and we weep. I read

the ancients, who had no names for
January or February, left them outside
the calendar. Days when the veil
between the living and dead
lifts a little, I like to think Grandma
lingers in those
empty months, waiting for me
on that bench.

Raccoon in the Night

I'd never struck
him before—well, that's
not quite true—one well

deserved spanking, but not
this: two men, rage-
flushed, I hit

hard, open-handed
in the chest and quick
as the horror

hit me, I felt
his light, bamboo
brittle, off-

balance body, pushed so
hard and far, how
many years

2

to make his way back? Seed
marauder, bandit
under the bird feeder, he

plays next to water's edge. I
can only imagine this. I never
actually see this creature. To come

upon him midday, I'd
be surprised
as if chance

should bring
my son and me together. Would we
stare before backing away

Larry Sorkin

3

into the woods. At the café
table, palm to palm, finger
tip to tip, something

we've done since
he was a kid, but this
is different. He repeats

that mine are longer,
thicker, still
thinking himself

the boy. Mine have retired
their length, strength while his
are a carpenter's: tool-

etched, dark-haired and finely
detailed. Even so,
I'm grateful, not

for relinquishing my place, too
stubborn for that, but for this healing,
this touch in the space between.

THAT

color. My family was that
shade: walls,
car, shirts, even
my eyes. Dad
said it was and so
it had to be, not a Gulf
Stream indigo, not
even a Bahamas' turquoise—this
was Wedgwood
pale: insipid
it seemed
to me as a kid, though
perhaps I just
resented that
color like family was imposed
without choice. My favorite,
I was told. While I
came to cherish this
family, I still won't
order that blue
plate special and have no
tolerance for
a robin's egg.

THE INITIATED

My bar mitzvah aftermath
tears, held
tight to Mom's chest, half
a century ago—the rabbi
pointed at strange
calligraphy with a gilt-silver
finger; I danced
with the just out-of-reach-too-
lovely Sherry R on the portable
dance floor in the Deauville
Hotel ballroom, her raised porcelain
right palm against my left, foxtrotting
into history. Supposed to be
a man, welcomed into
the mysterious
society of black coats to argue
all night over Talmudic paradox
of the soul. But, hoaxed, I'd made it
through my arcane Torah
portion mouthing Hebrew, understanding
bupkes, this first time at the *bimah* trying
to read from the scrolls would
be my last, just a gangly
boy with braces and plenty of reasons
to weep. Now when I sit with you
guys and one of us opens
a vein to the quick
silver current that carries
us along with Langston Hughes and last

night's dream lover and what can't
be said about a certain South
East Asian rice paddy, we move from
worlds of reason to tears, a boy
reading his portion behind
each of us men.

ALL NIGHT THE WIND

through the patio
door cracked open, sea

air across my salt-
tight skin until daybreak's

surprise—it wasn't just
Mom that made me; this

breath too blew me
into being: Kid Larry

thought the wind
would toughen his skin, asleep

on the deck, while the taut
anchor line vibrated

against its persistent
push, but instead

it opened him like
skate eggs dried,

broken and scattered
across the beach.

FROM THE PHOTOGRAPHIC

history of my mother spread
across the desk, infant

to grandma, the same in all
her evolutions; among

a hundred girls
in camp uniform, age 11

or 12, she jumps
out through decades, her

cherubic smile, full
cheeks, glint of hazel

eyes that even now
reminds her husband to sip

slowly from the warm
bowl of her tenderness. Almost

sixty years boils
down to this: *she gives,*

he takes and though
he's lost half

the weight of their
youth, there's enough

to nurture them
both on this last

day alone together.

Sty

In his concerned pediatrician
baritone, Dad asks Mom to put a boric

acid compress on my right
swollen eye. She boils ·

water, dips a teaspoon
of white powder from a cobalt

jar, stirs it in and pulls a clean
washcloth from the pantry

shelf. Next to me with the pot and soaked
wrapping on my bed, her weight

presses the mattress, pulling
us close. *Too hot*, I complain. *We'll just*

wait for it to cool, she whispers. As real
as this seems, it's hard not

to believe that in some parallel
infrared zone only a physicist

could fathom, she's still
beside me six

decades later as I lay this warm
compress over memory and feel

the wet heat.

Two Weeks in the Ground

I wouldn't want to bring
him back from interment even
if I could, but I wouldn't mind

repelling down to keep him
company, push
back the concrete

lid, climb into the tasteful
furniture that's become his
parlor and fill him in

on the gossip since
he checked out. Easier
to talk to now, I miss him

more than I imagined. Always
expecting his leaving would
set me free, surprised his new

silence and contained
grace leave me free enough
to grieve.

FATHER WAS THE SEA

When I was born, he
surrounded my island, at times rough,
forbidding or smooth like glass but
always vast and vanishing
toward who knows. When I was a boy,
he was a latched gate and whitewashed
high pickets through which everything
came and went. Then a desert
of hot days, cold nights and wavy
views across distance. Late on,
a forest of brambles
and steep, rocky hillsides, but also broad
trunks, hamlets
and creeks, much that was unseen
and light that filtered down
to the soft, leaf-moldy floor. When I died
he was the road.

YAHRZEIT

Up this a.m. to a bellowing
cow which must be a half
mile away and maybe

because of dew or window
open to spring, the wail
echoes around my bed announcing

that we all really do
know our fate. I'd like an upbeat
attitude making the best of this green

scene that comes
with the anniversary of Dad's
death: Easter and though He

rose again it's not
like He had an earthbound
afterlife beyond

crucifixion. This life/death
proximity, the contrast
is the thing. Yesterday's

drive home, a common
crow blocks my path tearing
into roadkill, staking out his

territory, his life pinned
to the spot the squirrel
lost his. The burning

wick, the one
extinguished and the difference
between.

Via Negativa

Not in the granite
headstone flush

with the ground, not
in the copper

bronze plate or the space left
between his arrival date

and departure, not
to be found in the new

constancy of Mother's
loneliness, or in my all the more

frequent reveries. What's left
of family meets

over Dad's grave, but not
over him. He's gone

from the direction he
would have given us, questions

he never answered and ones we haven't
come up with. Accustomed to not

finding him, he's not to be
found everywhere.

THE LAST LIVING

red oak along the entrance
road to my place isn't. Canopy

leaves turned brittle just
like the other half

dozen compatriots that
stood there barely

acknowledged through
my time here. Anita's husband

burned them for firewood
last winter. Ironic

I miss them more
in their leaving, like that grove

further down the road that withered
the year Dad died, imagine

them every time I stare through
the opening in the tree line.

DEATH IS DEAD

like a worn out 20's
East Side tenement that

should have been
bulldozed. So too

dead and *dying*, overused
like *love*

or *beauty*. I need
something fresh, the way the living

experience it. *Disappeared*
could work for how

they vanish, leaving only
a wake behind. Not

buried, that's just the trash
of them, maybe *ephemeral*, an idea for

what's taken form and gone. Mom's
gone and isn't, still coming

to mind, still
waiting for my call on Sunday

morning, catching
up on the weather: rainy patches

of mist in the hollow where
I can almost

make out a white tail retreating
beneath the pines.

THREE

SHE CALLS ME WHEN I'M OUT

of town to say she woke to her own
screams two nights in a row, those visions

lost to oblivion. I love
her honest

response to the dark. Had I—her hero
in woolens and nightcap—

been there, I would have
comforted, would have lied.

Larry Sorkin

CALL ME ADAM

This guy thinks he knows
love because he loves, like

a wave loves
the beach. Is he

wrong? Watch
him when she

walks out. Watch
him pace the long

night into daybreak as he stumbles
through empty rooms. Watch

him guard the cage
of his ribs with bare

arms that shelter the absence and that
heart drained by receding tide. Now

Adam, who
named the wooly

mammoth, the dodo and the carrier
pigeon, knows love.

DIPTYCH OF TWO EXES

Honey

she calls me at the end
of our conversation, and I recollect
a *sweetie* too along
with *dear* and some other
oldies that wouldn't have
been odd if
it hadn't been years since
we'd spoken. Not just
bitterness turning
it all strange
in my gut, there's a large
measure of sugar too left
in her singsong turning
of phrase that turns
the lock on the door
of an earlier version
of me I said goodbye to
maybe
thirty years ago.

Your Question

Of course I remember the mug:
two of them sporting
infusers to hold the tea
and a lid to retain heat, both
lovely—and you're right
one broke years ago while we
were together. Its poorly
mended unhealed
crack let light shine through, no
longer whole enough for
the comfort of tea. I still
stow it under a sink
cabinet tucked away in the back, kept
more now for what it was than
what it is. I believe the other
prettier one, unbroken, a garland
of pink flowers, a deep
basket for the limp leaves
and sharp slits to let water flow
through, was in your care, that I
had it packed up for you, carefully, but
if you don't have it then it must
have fled, searching for sanctuary
where it wouldn't
be broken or jostled: into
memory perhaps.

TWO SASSY WOMEN

like fear and fascination come
as twins in a red

coupe they abandon
in a ditch before

turning into gleaming
bronze scorpions. Down

the desert road they slink
into a storm drain; the clatter

of claws as they emerge from the other
side, restored beauties in fuck-me

pumps, amused and feigning
innocence. I watch, leaning

against my ride parked
up the street, while they shimmy

toward the glowing eye of my hand-
rolled smoke, their musky

perfume arriving just as I stub
ash against the sole

of my boot when this
dream fades to black.

Larry Sorkin

Owl

Reader, you don't
have to hear how
lonely I was for this
story or the state
of that divorce, it's all
there when I take you off
the blacktop down the dirt
road to the bungalow secreted
in the hollow where
I'd sit hours under the bare
bulb shining through the windowed
door into nothing, so
green, I'd never
seen a barn owl nor imagined
that ghost-faced
beast could hover
in the light blasting
the porch, not a clue what
had to die, what
wants to live, didn't
know fierceness could
penetrate from eye
to eye through the longest
stare since Jesus flew
to God from his perch.

FORGETTABLE

chat over a late Sunday salad with too
much wine until she fixed

me with her baby
blues and asked if I

was okay with how it turned
out—*it*? The vinaigrette or

"life" or our sixteen
years together could

be in play under the swinging bare
bulb interrogation. I tried to toss

it back with—*well, what
do you think?*—but she

refused to play, so I declared
I couldn't imagine being more

into it. She brought
a napkin to her lower

lip and seemed
satisfied. Me too, until the pitch

black now
of 4 a.m. wondering if

I even grasped her question
or my response.

Start Sideways with the Question

asked with a coy smile: if I
knew how eagles mate

and no, I didn't—so she
went on to describe

the way a pair
will circle and seize

each other, deadly
talons joined, spinning

toward earth, almost
coupling all the way

down, pulling out only
at the last, then

climb and restart this airy
passion. She

tells me catching
my eye with that wild

look just before she leans
sideways into the pillow.

THREE NIGHTS OF PRETEND WITH OWL

for Brenda

Forgive me. The truth
is the lie that on Monday night
I pretend to be with you but want
to be alone. I strip the Celtic
knot band from my ring finger
before we melt onto the distant
coasts of our king cradle. There will be no
pretense of love in sleep. Tuesday

night I drive to my mountain
cell where I pretend to
imitate myself pretending
to love solitude all
the while shooting
the breeze with you
in my head if not
over the phone. But this rare

Tuesday, I penetrate
the fantasy of my condition
in a single barred
owl's *who cooks*
for you, my breath visible
on the porch, ready

for Wednesday, hungry
for your olive
soup, grateful to wed
lock legs and fall
back into the middle of
our tender fiction.

Larry Sorkin

LOOSELY TIED

What thin breath holds me to all
this? My heart's uneven

rhythm? A balloon by a string
loosely tied to a child's

hand. This marriage
she and I have

honed, mostly common moments
strung together. Above

all, our beings wrap around
each other in this friendship. We pretend

permanence. Silk
scarf in a faint breeze.

CULPABLE NEGLIGENCE

That season again, and I'm lost
in mindless minutiae. I often don't
pay attention, but if

I remember to look
up, yellow poplar
leaves bud into goldfinch

plumage: still
mottled, they crowd
the feeder, then swoop

and bounce in flocks against
the sky, leaves that expand to catch
the light. As finches

transform into tulip
blossoms, poplars will go
full out. Wish

I had a lifetime of patience to spend
all day watching. How many
more springs? Twenty years

together this week, I've grown
used to her, too. Forgive me, sometimes
I forget to look.

What Falls from Heaven

In my flower bed I happen
on a white, deflated balloon and, tied
below, a ribbon and a rain-
worn wedding card. A barely
legible fragment from 1st Corinthians:

Love does not keep a record
of wrongs, does not delight
in evil, but rejoices, love always,
always…love never fails.

I wish for them what
they have wished and sent
up to heaven with such
lofty praise. Forgive the one
left holding this collapsed
rag of grandiose
hopes come to earth. Something
else must have
been written on my card, some
tragic/comic complication inscribed, for
I have a record
of injury and broken truths, no less
valuable to treasure in subtlety
and surprise. Is love that

absolute? I'm not, the love
I know would be less without
that other history, without some
certainty of how
fragile the petals.

THINK

of the way we build and then
rebuild on shaky ground: of San
Francisco collapsed
in rubble. We could argue how
foolish—don't we get what's
happened there, what will? Do we
rebuild because there's
nowhere else? Think
of fog sliding under that
iconic
bridge into the waiting
bay on the cool
evening held
through the night before it burns
off reluctant in the morning
heat. Of course you
and I would try
love again.

CHICAGO BREAKFAST

I sit; you talk; I polish
off your hash

browns; you spill
girl-juice excitement

sunny-side
yellow into my black

and bitter cup, now
a memory

of the sun not yet
stale behind my train

as it pulls
out into the night.

DOUBLETAKE

In the Burger
King lot wolfing

my still hot from
the grease BK

fish and battered
rings, I look twice

into the driver's side
van window in the next

space—Hollywood drive-in
vision of starlit

youth, she's straddling
him, mussed pageboy, back

to the steering wheel, flushed
cheeks pressed

to his, mouth taking
all she can get. I'm shocked, not

for the puritan or
the voyeur—I

could care less—it's me
decades ago, sin on a side street

with C steaming
up that rental, it's

me they wake
from the dead.

JUST

when I've relegated
libido to the Salvation
Army cast off
bin, buried
craving in the card
catalog of lost
languages, thought
I'd aged out of the gooey
slick of saliva, semen, what
have you,

you

insist on disabusing
me of my bubble
boy quarantine and pull
me into the salt
sea soak of skin
I was born in.

Pursuit

of a solitary
morning's ringside

seat to inhale
the ceaseless

erosion of this
folded Appalachian

ridge into a flat
plain interrupted by an Astaire

and Rogers pair of bluebirds that
tap dance on the porch

rail, each waving a single
wing to the other. I call my mate, a string

can line strung across seventy miles to share
a play by play of the ritual

as the male turns
away and she

waves and he
sings and waves and turns

back and so an hour
vanishes, while she and I

murmur our own
shorthand semaphore.

FOUR

BLACK STAR

The sun took
the wrong

road. The wealthy
are poor; the poor,

wise; the powerful,
impotent. The rest of us

watch from inside
the stone.

DREAM PAIRING: DESCENT

Bastet

Downstairs to find
the cat named for
an Egyptian goddess who's
picked up the poop
scoop in her deft
paws and proceeded
to methodically
clean
her litter box, saving yours
truly the pleasure. Just
a daydream, but
nonetheless I'm
impressed to catch
the profound masquerading
as the mundane
on a morning when
all I crave is to watch
the fescue
grow, and imagine
an afternoon not
cutting it.

Waking up

to descend
stairs barefoot, I'd
dreamt of running an
errand for Dad who had me
give away a Louisville
slugger and an orange
ball to a kid. Then I
remember he's
in a coma. No,
dead for years. Almost
awake, I decide to
bring this
dream to Henry
the shrink, but he
too is gone. Bastet stretched
out on my leg, claws
extended, holds
on tight.

TOENAILS

God takes the sweetest is supposed
to console or offer some
irony when a child
dies, but—if you live long enough—there
needs to be a measure
of vinegar. Henry had
some of that
hardness but became sweet
again too, like a child. His nails so
long it became difficult
to walk: he couldn't
reach to trim them. Dawn, a fitting
name for a nurse or angel, she'd
call him Mister
Henry, as in *Mister Henry, let me
cut them.* She soaked
his feet in a blue
plastic tub, moisturized
and massaged before
she clipped. He loved
her care, but in the hospice
ward when I held
his feet, the nails
had yellowed, become hard
and long again, as he
became soft and ready.

First Person Once Removed

Akin to laughter
but not. A whimper
maybe, like a half

starved mongrel, then downshift to
guttural, rhythmic;
the ribs

shake the strangest
sound ever that
echoes off the mirrored

shower, turns
to groans, sobs, sinks
to haunches, cries

muffled by splashing
rivulets that snake
to the drain. Thinks no

one's listening. Even
so, embarrassed by such
an outpouring, views another

naked, crouching and wet,
someone
else who got the call.

WHILE SHE SOBBED, MY WIFE

consoled, and I, call me
rude, from across the room
stared, awe struck, not at the public
raw emotion: she's leaving
town—difficult to move

from a place she'd grown
roots—surprised how
I envied her, hoping if
I were trailing Two
Men and a Truck or on my back in a pine

box, I'd want to weep
like that, to be that
connected to the love
and hate of a place. Fuck
holy detachment. Thirty

years ago, I fell face
first off a roof two stories onto a truck
fender and found myself on the temple
steps of the Other World—where I was turned
away. Let me

tell you, I was pissed, didn't
want to turn back. All these
years I've labored under
the misconception I was just
sticking it out here for another

chance to cross over. But
Huzzah! Poplars
outside my window
soak up February sun and can't
get enough. Neither

can I. Mom died. I won't
get over her. Grandma's name for me was
Momma's Boy, holding
on to her skirt. So
what, I'm attached. I wanted more

of her. When my son
picks up the phone and says *Hey
Pop*, I want more; when
my wife reaches across
the sheet to rest her fingertips

on my arm. That too. This
morning, if I don't get
struck down, I'll make a killer
omelet with fresh
tarragon and mushrooms, navel

slices, bagel, jasmine tea. I don't
want it to be my last but know
this, if it is, let no one
living say he wasn't holding
on for dear life.

READING OBITS

Reminds me of an application's
not so pertinent

facts: birth, address, next
of kin, which brings me

to the pieces I'd like left
out of mine, the dozen or more

occupations I struggled at, never
to master: paranoid teenage

purveyor of dime bags, hack
sign painter, skinny ass nude

model…what about my grand
list of exes or the son who

at times would have preferred not
to be mentioned? While I'm at it, what's

the point of the all-too-brief
epitaph or dates

of coming and going? What should
be chiseled: *He Was Here,*

He's Gone? Whatever
value there was, whatever

crept onto my page in this
book of brief loving, will

be a life burned
away in the fire of living it.

I HAVE NOTHING

this morning, bits
of nothing found among the clean

stones that pepper the drive where two
tiny sky-blue eggs crack open. One

empty, not quite dry. I lift
with thumb and forefinger as it

crumbles to my clumsy
touch. I leave the other, half

full of liquid sun. How
fragile the chance of what

gets to breathe
and sing. I carry the broken

bits back on my right
palm held open, outstretched, an

offering. I carry them
to you, Reader, before this

world as we know it sinks
like a skipping

stone below a cosmic
wave.

What's Worth Saving

Not the ratty thirty-year-old
shirt, not

the worn, wine-stained
ottoman or the steaming

heat of this July morning. On the fence
about the remembered

fights with the ex, or
plunging into suicidal

gloom: could I have this without
that? Should I cast

a cold eye on these
thousand or so feeble attempts

at verse only to keep
one out of ten—but how

that one sings. I can still
hear Henry say
as I leave the page: *Be good*

to yourself, and Babe,
I grip tight

that smile in your voice when I
slip the key

in the lock and come
home to you.

FLUNKING OUT IN ADVENTURELAND

It could have hit me
finding my picture on the front
page of the business section's latest

walk of shame or the pronouncement
of a wife as she, suitcase
in hand, flips me off on her way

out the door, but last night
it came whispered by the ghost
of my dear Henry

in a deathbed dream, *Whatever odd*
life goal brought you to this
planet, whatever divine mission imagined

on the back of a white steed, you'll never
achieve it. How could it be
otherwise? Ambition—that bejeweled

temptress—isn't
the type to be satisfied; this
isn't the nobility

Disney promised. Friend, I've come
to the truth late, hoodooed
by the occasional mirage

of success. Maybe
it's shock, but I'm nothing
more than a guy getting old

rocking an afternoon
on the porch eyeballing
forever

spring clouds. Litany
from the unfinished
stack on my desk slips

into nothing while
thoughts of the consequence
of failure drift away—drawn, as I

haven't been since God only
knows how young, to look
into the cumulus

wonder and find the ears
of a talking mouse drifting
across the heavens.

About the Author

 Larry Sorkin is a some-of-the-time North Carolina poet, a part-time businessman and an occasional performer of poetry with the classical music group, The Bechtler Ensemble. He presents workshops exploring the connections between poetry and fine arts, dance, music and depth psychology. He is a summer poet-in-residence at the Airy Knoll Arts Project. Poetry didn't come to Sorkin until his forties when he fell under the infectious influence of Robert Bly. He considers it a calling to spread the passion. He often holes up on his ridgetop overlooking the Piedmont, daydreaming into the fields and onto paper.

All author's proceeds from this book will be donated to charity.

bonhomie 🍐 press

Bonhomie Press, an imprint of Mango Publishing, publishes inspiring and distinctive fiction and memoir. Mango Publishing , established in 2014, publishes an eclectic list of books by diverse authors— both new and established voices—on topics ranging from business, personal growth, women's empowerment, LGBTQ studies, health, and spirituality to history, popular culture, time management, decluttering, lifestyle, mental wellness, aging, and sustainable living. Mango was recently named 2019 *and* 2020's #1 fastest growing independent publisher by *Publishers Weekly*. Our success is driven by our main goal, which is to publish high quality books that will entertain readers as well as make a positive difference in their lives.

Our readers are our most important resource; we value your input, suggestions, and ideas. We'd love to hear from you—after all, we are publishing books for you!

Please stay in touch with us and follow us at:

Facebook: Mango Publishing
Twitter: @MangoPublishing
Instagram: @MangoPublishing & @YellowPearPress
LinkedIn: Mango Publishing
Pinterest: Mango Publishing
Newsletter: mangopublishinggroup.com/newsletter

Join us on Mango and Bonhomie's journey to reinvent publishing, one book at a time.